EUREKA!
Stories of Everyday Inventions

PHILIP BRYAN
Illustrated by Mark Payne

Written by Philip Bryan
Illustrated by Mark Payne
  Xiangyi Mo (wheels, page 15)
Designed by Peter Shaw

Published by Mimosa Publications Pty Ltd
PO Box 779, Hawthorn 3122, Australia
© 1995 Mimosa Publications Pty Ltd
All rights reserved

Literacy 2000 is a Trademark registered in the United States Patent and Trademark Office.

Distributed in the United States of America by

Rigby
  A Division of Reed Elsevier Inc.
  500 Coventry Lane
  Crystal Lake, IL 60014
  800-822-8661

Distributed in Canada by
  PRENTICE HALL GINN
  1870 Birchmount Road
  Scarborough
  Ontario M1P 2J7

03 02 01 00
10 9 8 7 6
Printed in China through Bookbuilders

ISBN 0 7327 1577 6

CONTENTS

What Is an Invention? 4
EUREKA! 4

Fast Foods 6
HOT DIGGETY DOG! 6
THE THIN EDGE OF THE WEDGE 7
AN ACE MEAL 8
A HEALTHY DREAM 10
WHAT A DRIP! 11

Fun Time 12
BITS AND PIECES 12
A SMASH HIT 14
NEVER A CROSS WORD 16

Getting It Together 18
HOOKED IN 18
ZIPPITY-DOO-DAH 20
PINNING IT DOWN 22
THE TROUSERS THAT REALLY WORKED 24

The Write Stuff 26
THE WRITING STICK 26
A STICKY SOLUTION 28
BOOKS 30

EUREKA!

What Is an Invention?

People have been discovering and inventing things for thousands of years. And sometimes brain waves happen in the strangest places! The Greek scientist Archimedes lived about 2200 years ago. As he sat in his tub one day, he noticed that the water had risen. The changing water level showed how much space his body was taking up in the water.

Archimedes had been puzzling over a problem that the bathtub experience suddenly helped him to solve – how to measure the volume of gold and silver objects, even if they had very irregular shapes. He was so excited that he jumped out of the bathtub, without getting dried or dressed, and ran down the street shouting "Eureka!" (I found it!) And the expression caught on!

Inventing means creating something new. Of the hundreds of things we use each day, some were invented accidentally, while others were the result of years of development. Many inventions were dreams that became reality through hard work; one was even someone's way of paying off a debt! Some inventions were so new and different when they were created that no one knew what to do with them.

HOT DIGGETY DOG!

Hot dogs started life as frankfurters, a kind of sausage from Frankfurt, Germany. They had been popular all over Germany for about 800 years, and when German immigrants came to the United States, one of the things they brought with them was their taste for frankfurters. Frankfurter sausages soon became popular in their new home, too. In 1900, vendors at New York baseball games started calling them "hot dachshund sausages" because their long skinny shape looked like a dachshund dog. But people found it too hard to say, "A hot dachshund with mustard, please," and the name was soon shortened to "hot dog."

Fast Foods

THE THIN EDGE OF THE WEDGE

Potato chips, or crisps, were invented in 1853 by George Crum, a Native American who was a chef in Saratoga Springs, New York.

One day a customer in the restaurant where Crum worked complained that the french fries were too thick and not salty enough. Crum was very angry about this and, in a fury, he cut some potatoes into wafer thin slices, fried them in oil, and covered the chips in salt. He waited in the kitchen, expecting the customer to say that they were "*too* salty," or "*too* thin." But, to Crum's surprise, the customer loved them! These "Saratoga Chips" quickly became a popular snack.

Today, chips are still very popular in many parts of the world and are available in dozens of different varieties and flavors.

AN ACE MEAL

Sandwiches are named after the Earl of Sandwich, an English nobleman of the eighteenth century. The Earl of Sandwich loved playing cards. In fact, he loved playing cards so much that he didn't want to stop to eat! One day, when he was halfway through a card game, he asked his servant to bring him a slice of roast beef between two slices of bread. For the Earl, this was ideal – a meal you could hold in one hand while you played cards with the other! Today millions of people eat sandwiches for lunch!

DID YOU KNOW?

Not everybody eats sandwiches, but almost everybody eats some form of bread. Bread is the most widely eaten food in the world and it has been around for thousands of years. It is made from grains such as wheat or rye and is often flat, as it is in India, where it is called *chapatti*.

A HEALTHY DREAM

Breakfast cereals were invented by an American named John Kellogg. Kellogg ran a health farm and was always thinking about new ways of making healthy food appetizing. He must have thought that people wanted a change from soggy oatmeal for breakfast, because it was his great dream to create a crisp, flaked, breakfast cereal. And he did have a dream about it!

One night, Kellogg dreamed of the perfect way to make a breakfast cereal. When he woke up, he leaped out of bed and went straight to his kitchen, where he boiled some wheat, rolled it into strips, and baked it in the oven, just as he had done in his dream.

Kellogg served his new cereal to people visiting his health farm, and they all seemed to like it. In fact, one of the visitors liked it so much that he started to make and sell his own cereal. Soon a lot of other people had copied the idea, too. By the time Kellogg started producing cornflakes in 1907, there were already 44 other companies producing breakfast cereal!

WHAT A DRIP!

Although the Chinese had begun making iced desserts at least 800 years ago, the ice-cream cone wasn't invented until this century.

At the World's Fair in St. Louis in 1904, a young woman was eating ice cream served between two wafers. It was a warm day, so she wrapped the wafers around the ice cream in a cone shape to prevent it from dripping onto her clothes. This clever action was seen by several people, one of whom was a waffle maker. Soon he was turning waffles into ready-made cones. They became extremely popular, and the ice-cream cone was born!

WOW, THAT'S *REALLY COOL!*

BITS AND PIECES

Fun Time

Jigsaws can be fun – and educational, too! The first jigsaw was invented by a schoolteacher who wanted to help his pupils learn their geography. John Spilsbury, who was teaching in England in 1760, knew that his students hated learning the names of mountains, rivers, and capital cities.

Spilsbury glued a map of England onto a thin sheet of wood, then used a fine saw, called a jigsaw, to cut the map along the borders of the different counties. His pupils had fun piecing the puzzle together and learning their geography at the same time.

Today, you don't usually learn geography while you are doing a jigsaw – but you still need to be observant and patient.

There are jigsaws with as few as three pieces, and some with as many as 150,000!

DID YOU KNOW?

The first teddy bear was made by a German dressmaker, Margarete Steiff. In 1903, three thousand cuddly bears were imported to America, where they soon became very popular. They were later called Teddy Bears after President Theodore Roosevelt. The teddy bear is still one of the world's best-loved toys.

A SMASH HIT

If you thought roller skates were a modern invention, you were wrong! They first appeared in 1760. When Joseph Merlin, a Belgian, was invited to a ball in London in 1760, he decided that he wanted to stand out from the crowd. But what could he do to grab people's attention? He thought of walking in playing the violin, but decided that wasn't spectacular enough.

Finally, he attached wheels to his shoes, tucked his violin under his arm, and rolled in!

Merlin had invented the first roller skates! Unfortunately, he only discovered as he rolled into the ballroom that the skates were very good at rolling in a straight line, but very difficult to turn or stop. There was a stunned hush as Merlin rolled rapidly across the ballroom… and crashed straight into a large mirror, smashing it! Roller skates have changed a lot since Merlin's smash hit. Boots are now attached to the skates and the wheels are often made of plastic. In-line skates are the latest version of Merlin's invention.

DID YOU KNOW?

No one knows who invented the first wheel, but we do know that wheels have been around for more than 5000 years. Early wheels were made of wood and were probably sliced off the end of a tree trunk. Solid wheels were heavier than wheels with spokes, which were developed 4000 years ago.

NEVER A CROSS WORD

What has four letters and is found at the seashore? If you guessed *sand*, then you have just solved one of the clues in the first ever crossword. Crosswords were invented in 1913 by an Englishman named Arthur Wynne. He worked for an American newspaper and was always looking for new puzzles to fill the games page. He based his "word-cross puzzle," as he called it, on an old game called Magic Square.

He used black squares to show where letters weren't needed, and 32 simple word definitions as clues. Wynne had invented the crossword, but it wasn't until 1924, when a book of crossword puzzles was published, that the crossword craze really began.

DID YOU KNOW?
Paper was invented in China more than 1800 years ago. The first paper was made from the inner bark of the mulberry tree. Paper gets its name from *papyrus*, a reed the ancient Egyptians used for making writing material.

HOOKED IN

Getting It Together

Have you ever gone walking in the countryside and had prickles stick to your clothes? If you have, then you could have invented velcro! After walking in the mountains one day in 1948, George de Mestral, a Swiss man, noticed that he had burrs (tiny seed pods) stuck all over his socks and trousers. When he looked more closely, he discovered that each burr had hooks that caught on the fibers in his clothing.

De Mestral decided to invent a fastener that worked like a burr. He experimented for eight years before he perfected his invention: two pieces of tape, one with thousands of hooks, and the other with thousands of loops. He combined the words "velvet" and "crochet" (the French word for "hook") to give his invention a name. Today, velcro is used to fasten jackets, sports shoes, and even space suits.

ZIPPITY-DOO-DAH

The zipper was invented because of a bad back! In 1893, most people wore button-up boots. This was a problem for people with bad backs; bending down to do up all the buttons could cause a lot of pain. An American, Whitcombe Judson, invented what he called a "hookless fastener" so that one of his friends, who had bad back pain, could fasten his boots in one movement.

Judson's invention was not a big success at first – it kept coming undone at the wrong time! In 1913, a Swedish inventor named Gideon Sundback improved Judson's design. The new, improved style was used to close flying suits and snow boots. When pilots found that they could close their flying suits with one *zip* of the hand, they started calling the fasteners "zippers."

DID YOU KNOW?
No one knows when people first used buttons, but we do know that the early Greeks and Romans used them for fastening with loops, and as decoration. It wasn't until the 1200s, when fitted clothes became popular, that the buttonhole was invented to go with the button!

PINNING IT DOWN

The modern safety pin was invented to pay off a debt! William Hunt, an American inventor, had borrowed $15 that he couldn't pay back. In 1849, that was more than a week's wages! The man to whom Hunt owed the money offered to cancel the debt, *and* pay Hunt more than $400 if he could bend a piece of wire into a useful object.

After three hours of bending and twisting, Hunt had created a safety pin. Actually, it wasn't a new invention so much as a *re*invention. People in Europe had used a similar type of pin to fasten their cloaks 4000 years earlier. Today, versions of Hunt's invention are found just about everywhere – and he sold the rights for only $400!

THE TROUSERS THAT REALLY WORKED

Levi Strauss was a German who immigrated to America last century. When the gold rush started in California in 1849, Strauss decided that, rather than search for gold, he would make his fortune selling tent canvas to miners. He soon discovered that most of the miners already had tents and weren't interested in buying his canvas. But what they did need were work trousers that wouldn't rip or tear.

Strauss began making and selling trousers. He used canvas at first, and then a fabric imported from Genoa, Italy. The Italian name of this fabric later came to be pronounced as "jean" and trousers made from it were called "jeans." Trousers bearing Levi's brand are still being worn today. In fact, jeans are one of the most popular garments in the world and are worn in nearly every country!

DID YOU KNOW?
The first sewing machine was patented by Thomas Saint, an Englishman, in 1790. It was wooden, and used only a single thread to stitch leather.

THE WRITING STICK

As a journalist, Laszlo Biro, a Hungarian, needed to write fast, accurate notes. He wasn't impressed with his fountain pen because it left blotches and often had to be refilled. In 1938, after experimenting for some time with different designs, Laszlo and his brother George developed a new pen. It contained a tube filled with thin ink that would dry as soon as it was exposed to air, and a tiny metal ball at the end of the tube, to help control the flow of the ink.

The Write Stuff

DID YOU KNOW?
Ink was used by the Chinese and the Egyptians as early as 2500 BC. It was made from a variety of natural materials such as berries, bark, and soot.

INK IN A PLASTIC TUBE

The Biro brothers called their invention a "non-leaking writing stick"– but their "sticks" didn't sell very well at first. They were expensive, and at first no one could see a use for them – until British and U.S. pilots in World War Two found that, unlike fountain pens, they didn't leak at high altitudes. Ballpoint pens were introduced to the public in 1945, when a New York department store sold 10,000 in one day – at twelve dollars each!

INK FLOWS ONTO A SMALL METAL BALL

A STICKY SOLUTION

Spencer Silver was working in a research laboratory in 1970 when he discovered a strange sort of glue – it stuck, but not permanently. The problem with Silver's glue was that no one knew what to do with it!

It was ten years before Arthur Fry, who worked with Silver, found a use for the mystery glue. Fry sang in a choir, and he wanted to find a way to mark pages in his music book without damaging the paper. He put a thin layer of the glue onto page markers and attached them to the book. Perfect! With the help of Silver's sticky invention, he had invented removable labels – sticky bits of paper that can be stuck, unstuck, and stuck again.

Pancake Recipe
up plain flour
2 eggs
inch of salt
3/4 cups of milk

Return library book

Remember to bring the beans

Take Albert for a walk

DO NOT OPEN !!

Radioactive socks!

Feed the Goldfish

orrow Frogs' book

Don't forget homework!

tennis gear

MARCO'S FOR LUNCH SATURDAY!

SPORTS SHOES

KEEP OUT PRIVATE BEDROOM

Count the tadpoles. Any froglets yet?

Big game Tuesday night

DID YOU KNOW?
The earliest pencils date back to the ancient Greeks and Egyptians, who used flat cakes of lead to mark lines on papyrus. The first modern pencil, consisting of a wooden case glued around a stick of graphite, was developed in the late 1700s.

BOOKS

No one actually invented the first book. Books developed over thousands of years, as people improved on or adapted inventions from many different places and different times.

Before modern paper was invented, people all over the world developed different materials to write on. Thousands of years ago in Ancient Egypt, people used a sort of paper made from papyrus reeds, and they made "books" in the form of scrolls; in Babylon, pieces of clay were baked hard and used to record information; in China, writing was done on bamboo or strips of wood; and in India, palm leaves were used.

Can you imagine writing a whole book by hand? That is what happened in Europe until the 1400s! Professional writers, called scribes, spent their days copying religious books.

THIS CENTRAL AMERICAN CODEX (AN EARLY BOOK) WAS MADE BY PAINTING ON DEER-SKIN.

The printing of the kind of books we are familiar with was made possible by the development, in the 1400s, of alphabet letters made of metal which could be moved around to make words. These metal letters were then coated in ink and pressed against paper. Johannes Gutenberg, working in Germany, developed the first printing press, and in 1456 the first "real" printed book appeared!

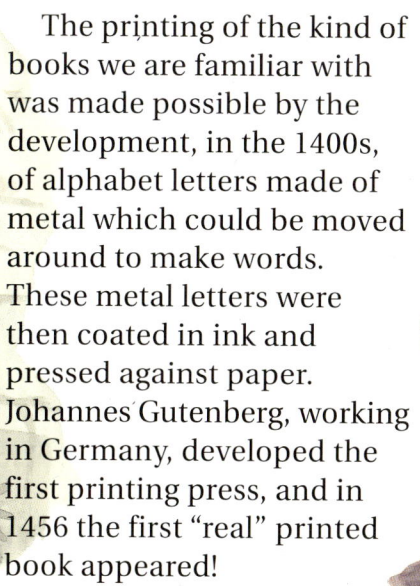

MMM... GREAT IDEA

These days, we use computers to move letters around to make the words in a book, and a modern printing press can produce thousands of books in one day!

TITLES IN THE SERIES

SET 10A

A Battle of Words
The Rainbow Solution
Fortune's Friend
Eureka
It's a Frog's Life

SET 10B

The Cat Burglar of Pethaven Drive
The Matchbox
In Search of the Great Bears
Many Happy Returns
Spider Relatives

SET 10C

Horrible Hank
Brian's Brilliant Career
Fernitickles
It's All in Your Mind, James Robert
Wing High, Gooftah

SET 10D

The Week of the Jellyhoppers
Timothy Whuffenpuffen-
 Whippersnapper
Timedetectors
Ryan's Dog Ringo
The Secret of Kiribu Tapu Lagoon

Acknowledgments:
Allsport: Mike Powell (skater, cover, page 15). ***Australian Picture Library:*** (early airplane and car, early washing machine, lamp, gramophone and record, fan, peg, page 5; button-up boot, page 21). ***Alan Gillard:*** (bread, pages 8-9). ***The Image Bank:*** *Nancy Brown* (children in jeans, page 25). ***David Johns:*** (chips, cover, page 7; ballpoint pen, cover, page 27; jigsaw, cover, page 13; shoe, cover, page 19; cornflakes, page 10; velcro, page 19; zipper, buttons, pages 20-21; girl with hat, page 22; back of badge, page 22; safety pin, pages 22-23; bandaged hand, page 23; writing instruments, page 26; removable labels, pages 28-29). ***The Photo Library:*** *Leslie Harris* (ham sandwich, page 9). ***Stock Photos:*** *John Oxley Library* (workers in jeans, page 25). ***The Stock Market:*** *John Paul Endress* (ice cream, page 11). ***The Werner Forman Archive:*** (book, page 30).